FAMILY TREE

ANGELA GRIFFITHS

HUTCHINSON

London Melbourne Sydney Auckland Johannesburg

Hutchinson Education

An imprint of Century Hutchinson Ltd

62-65 Chandos Place, London WC2N 4NW

Century Hutchinson Australia Pty Ltd
PO Box 496, 16-22 Church Street, Hawthorn, Victoria 3122, Australia

Century Hutchinson New Zealand Ltd
PO Box 40-086, Glenfield, Auckland 10, New Zealand

Century Hutchinson South Africa (Pty) Ltd
PO Box 337, Bervlei 2012, South Africa

First published 1984
Reprinted 1986, 1987

© Angela Griffiths 1984

Photoset in Times Roman by
Kelly Typesetting Ltd, Bradford-on-Avon, Wiltshire

Printed and bound in Great Britain by
Anchor Brendon Ltd, Tiptree, Essex

British Library Cataloguing in Publication Data
Griffiths, Angela
   Family tree.—(Ace series)
   1. Readers
   I. Title
   428.6'2   PE1119

ISBN 0 09 154621 4

Other titles in the *Aces* Series

Stories

Ellen's Week   Sue Wright
Long Gone Lil   Angela Griffiths
The Chaplin Story   Madeline Sotheby
Bold as Brass   Jan Mark
The Silent Scream   Terry Deary
Dear Stan . . .Yours Pete   Angela Griffiths
The Bob Marley Story   Madeline Sotheby

Plays

No Good at Games   David Williams
Rings a Bell   Angela Griffiths

1

It was a Saturday at the start of the summer holiday. Just a normal kind of Saturday. The kind that fits between Friday and Sunday. I was in the front garden, cleaning the engine of my bike. I'd had a good dinner and the sun was warm on my back. My whippet dog was snoring on the grass. Peace, perfect peace. Until a strange grunting sound made me turn. And there was Gran climbing a long wooden ladder. I wouldn't have taken any notice – but this ladder was up against the great beech tree in the road outside our house!

I called and ran to stop her. I tried to climb up after her. But too late. All I got was a pink fluffy slipper in my face. Gran is stubborn. Once she's made up her mind to do a thing, she will do it. No matter what! That's what makes her so hard to live with. (She came to us for a holiday five years ago – and stayed. Our house has never been the same since.)

At the top of the ladder Gran stopped. But only long enough to pop a sweet in her mouth. I peered through oily fingers. I was afraid to look in case she fell. Her bony knees were level with the top rung now. She was hanging on to a branch. Just like an overgrown sparrow. But she was not as weak as she looked. There was a certain light in her eyes. I knew that light. It was the light of battle.

'Mind out of the way, Charlie,' she yelled down to me. Then she kicked the ladder away from the tree. I stepped aside as it fell. It landed with a loud thud on the grass. Something white flew across the garden. It was the dog going indoors – scared stiff.

Now it was quiet. There was just the sound of Gran's heavy breathing and her after-dinner burp. This was her answer to Greenvale Town Council. The Council had passed plans to cut down the trees and make our road wider. But Gran had plans of her own.

She had already had one fight with a Council workman. Only a week ago she had marched out to the road and hit him with a leg of lamb. Lucky for him he was wearing his yellow safety helmet at the time. The poor man was only doing his job. He was painting a cross on each tree, marking them ready for coming down. But Gran soon sorted him out. She told him the beech trees were over 100 years old and it was her duty to protect the trees – even if it meant a fight to the death! Gran against the town planners. My money was on Gran.

I groaned as Gran climbed to the next branch. She was now almost halfway up the tree. I yelled at her but she did not answer. She was in a world of her own. I offered to make her a cup of tea. I told her the dog would pine and starve. (She loves Spindle, our whippet.) But there was still no answer. I reminded her that there was an old film on TV that evening. She likes films which date back to the year dot, or double-dot. I offered to clean my room . . . clean her room . . . clean any room. I even offered to cut her toe-nails. But it was no good. Gran would not be bribed.

The sun was full in my eyes. My back was damp with sweat. I began to feel edgy. Why did Gran have to protect the trees? Why the big deal? Why couldn't she just go away and find a nice hobby. Shark-fishing maybe.

2

I could feel my heart thumping every time Gran moved. Just to make things worse, I was on my own with the problem. Mum and Dad were away in Bristol, staying with Aunt Brenda for the weekend and my young brother and sister were away at summer camp. Which left just me and one whippet. I thought about ringing for the Police. Or the Ambulance Service. Or the Fire Service. Or all three. I didn't know what to do. I had a sudden wish to join the Army. That's the effect Gran has.

Gran's foot slipped. A twig cracked. My heart missed a beat. And a shower of mint toffees fell. Gran pulled herself up and hung on to a branch. She had very nearly fallen. I wanted her to come down – but not that quick!

'Gran, will you listen to me,' I said.

'I might listen. I might not,' said Gran.

I stepped nearer to the tree. I slapped a hand on the bark. The paint was still tacky where it was marked for coming down. As if I needed reminding.

'You had better listen, or there will be big trouble,' I said. 'Any minute now, someone is bound to ring for the Police. So come down now. Before it's too late!'

No answer from Gran. Not a word.

I tried again. 'Please come down, Gran. I'll help you save all the trees in the road. I'll collect names. I'll help you write letters to your MP. I'll do anything. But come down now!'

Gran turned. She was looking pleased with herself. She had found a place for herself in a cleft of the tree. It was like a small platform. Just over halfway up, where the trunk divides. I hoped she would not get a sudden giddy turn. She was high now.

On a level with my attic bedroom window.

She grinned down at me. Then she said, 'I can't hear anything you say, Charlie, because of the breeze.'

There was no breeze. There wasn't even a breath of fresh air. The heatwave was now in its second week.

I walked round the tree. And back again. I felt worried. And angry. And scared. Things were really getting out of hand now. If only I could turn back the clock. I just wanted life to be normal again.

I thought of all the things that usually drive me mad. Things like Gran's teeth clicking at meals. And Gran's hair pins in the bath. And Gran's boiled tripe stinking the house out. None of them seemed quite so bad now. At least they were things you could keep private. But a Gran in a tree could never be kept private. Not in a small town like Greenvale. (Population three thousand – and that's counting the back-yard hens.) I would be the laugh of the year if this got into the papers. It would be worse still if my mates at Tech college found out. There was a new girl in my engineering class. Her name was Tessa. I was fond of her and hoping she would grow fond of me. I planned to ask her out when the time was right. But after this there probably would not be a right time. Madness in the family would be a real turn-off.

Gran was sitting now. Grinning from ear to ear. Unpacking her apron pockets. I counted five small apples and a bag of toffees. Plus cake. It looked as though she planned to stay up for some while.

I walked round the ladder which was flat down on the grass. I began to think hard. Would it be a good idea to put the ladder up . . . then climb up . . . and drag Gran down by force? A quick raid,

11

then all over. I could do it. Easily. I was twice the size of Gran. Well, almost. I could use Commando shock tactics. Neat and nimble. Finished in a jiffy. But the thought of my teeth stopped me. Gran would probably kick them in.

The town clock was striking the hour. I checked it with my watch. Three o'clock. Mick and the gang would be down in the market square now, revving up their bikes, ready to hit the road. They might wait five minutes for me. But they wouldn't wait long. They're not the waiting type.

I went to put the cover on my bike.

'Gran, I'm sick of you!' I said, suddenly.

Gran waved me away. 'Go on. Go with your mates if you want to. There's no need for you to stay here.'

I frowned up at her. How could I go? I couldn't just leave her halfway up a tree. I had to stay – and she knew it!

'If you stay in that tree you'll be very sorry,' I said.

I tried to make it sound like an awful warning. But my voice cracked. Next door a curtain twitched. Any minute now there would be trouble with our neighbour. I rubbed my eyes. The sun was making them ache. My neck ached too. So did my head. Life was one big ache.

I looked along the road. Lorries and a tractor stood ready for work to begin on Monday. Then I had one more try. 'You can't stay there because that tree is coming down in two days time.'

As usual Gran had the last word. 'This tree only comes down over my dead body – and I'm not dying yet!'

3

I was right. Our neighbour was angry. Very angry indeed. Her name is Miss Gerkin. She's got a face like a ferret, and she throws all her garden snails over our hedge. No sooner had she replaced her curtains than she was out in her garden. With her hands on her hips, and spitting fire, she said, 'Your grandmother should be ashamed of herself . . . she lowers the tone of this road . . . she needs locking away . . . she shouldn't be allowed out . . . it's a downright disgrace!' She made her speech. Then she was gone.

This was followed by a visit from the three little girls who live at number ten. They thought it was a huge joke to see Gran up a tree. They laughed so much they almost choked. (Poor little dears.) 'Look at Charlie's funny Gran,' they said. And 'Look at the funny monkey.' Then they skipped round and round the tree singing a song. It was a rude song about Charlie Barley and his Grotty Granny. So I told them to go. Or else! They said they were only trying to be friendly. And just to prove it the smallest one kicked me on the shin.

The Police arrived just as I was limping indoors. The car screeched to a halt at the foot of the tree and two policemen got out. They both looked grim. The way they're trained to look. They both slammed their car doors. The way they're trained to slam doors. One was a real giant. He must have been seven feet tall or more. The other was a heavy type. Built like a steam roller. Only faster.

The tall one fixed me with a steely stare. He walked towards me. Then he was down. Sprawled flat on the ground. He had tripped over the ladder which was hidden by grass. I pretended not to notice. But a trickle of sweat was running down my back. And my face seemed frozen, like rock. When the policeman stood up he looked even grimmer. His mouth had taken on a new shape – like a slice of melon the wrong way up.

'What's going on here?' he asked.

As he spoke a mint toffee fell. It missed him by inches. He looked up sharply. When he saw Gran his mouth dropped open and he stood like a surprised guppy fish.

Gran smiled. Friendly as ever. 'Good evening, Officer,' she said. 'I am squatting in this tree, as you see.'

The policeman peered up at Gran for about half a minute. It seemed like half a year. Then he said, 'Squatting in trees is not allowed.'

Gran peered back down at him. 'Why? Is there a law against it?'

The heavy one stepped forward. 'Madam, I must ask you to come down from that tree. Come down now!'

Gran shook her head. 'I'm sorry. I can't come down. I'm up here to do a protest.'

The two men closed ranks. They felt there was safety in numbers. Then the tall one asked Gran why she was protesting. Gran needed no prompting. She told the men all about the plan to cut down the trees in Park Road. Cutting down a live tree was akin to murder, she said. And she could not allow murder. Besides, if Park Road had no trees it would soon be as busy as the M1. If the Council wanted to move the trees they would have to move her first . . . and so on . . . and so on.

I don't think the policemen had met a case like this before. They stood frowning at each other. Then they both frowned at me.

Gran called down, 'This has nothing to do with Charlie, my grandson. So leave him out of it.' She then asked the men if they liked trees. When they said yes she told them to go and join the Special Branch. They were not amused.

The tall one took out his notebook. He turned the pages slowly, as if he had all the time in the world. Then he began to ask questions, fast. There were lots of questions. He even wanted to know the name of our whippet.

A toffee paper floated down. Gran was getting edgy. I could tell by the way she was using her sweets. Chain-chewing. The two men stared at the ladder in the grass. One of them kicked the ladder and said 'Ouch.' They were both thinking hard. Then the heavy one spoke to Gran in a kind way. He called her 'love' and asked her to come down quietly. He said he wanted all of us to sort out the problem indoors, over a cup of tea. But Gran said no thanks, she would stay right where she was until the Council promised to leave our trees alone.

The sound of a sniff came through the garden hedge. Miss Gerkin, our neighbour, was listening to everything. Poking her nose into our lives, as usual. I felt hot under the collar in more ways than one.

I waited as the two policemen went into a huddle. Then one suggested calling the Fire Service. This annoyed Gran: down came another shower of toffee papers . . . and leaves . . . and twigs.

'Go away! Leave me in peace!' yelled Gran.

'We can't leave you up in a tree. You must come down,' said the tall one.

'I will not come down,' said Gran.

'You will!' said the heavy one.

'Will not.'

'You will!'

'Will not!'

I stepped forward quickly. 'Gran, please. . . .'

'You stay out of this, Charlie.'

Gran was furious now. Her face had turned a funny shade of plum. She was kneeling. Fists clenched. 'How high do you think this tree is?' she said, suddenly, to the men.

We all gazed up. Then the tall one said, 'I reckon that tree must be almost a hundred feet high.'

Gran stood. Then she began to chant. It went something like this:

'If I climb up high, as high as the sky,
Will I float and fly? Or fall and die!'

She then made a speech. A speech about trees and people and freedom. And she asked the policemen to go. Nicely but firmly. She warned them that if they did not go she would have to climb upwards to find some peace. She also warned them of the awful mess there would be on the roof of their car – if she fell from the top of the tree.

They got the message. They left in a hurry. Slam! Slam! I waited until their car had turned the corner at the end of the road. Then I flopped. My legs felt like two yards of tape.

Gran was not a bit worried. I could hear her cackling up in the tree like a happy old hen. She was feeling pleased with herself. Proud of herself. But I knew the Police would be back. Gran may have won the first round. But the fight was only just beginning.

4

The rest of Saturday was like a bad dream. No sooner had the Police gone than the Press arrived. They came by push-bike. One boy reporter and a spotty girl with a camera. The sun was low in the sky when they arrived. But the air was still warm. Warm and stuffy. It was hard to breathe. I could smell bonfires somewhere. Like old tyres burning. But it may have been the girl's perfume.

The reporter was full of questions. Who was the old woman in the tree? What was she doing up there? Why did she go up? When did she go up? How did she go up?

At first I said 'No comment'. Just to shut him up. But then he wore me down. So I told him about Gran's fight with the Council. Just to get him off my back.

The daylight was almost gone. But that did not stop the girl taking photos. Click . . . click . . . click. This way and that. I think she was powered by electric motor. She took one photo of the beech tree. One of Gran dangling a leg. One of our house. One of me with a hand in front of my face. And one of her own left foot. (That last one was a mistake. She tripped on the ladder.) Gran was quiet – until the reporter began to lift the ladder. Then, Gran gave him a piece of her mind. The worst piece. And he dropped the ladder back on the grass.

'You had better go,' I told the reporter. 'My grandmother is getting angry – and when she's angry anything can happen.' The reporter wrote down what I said in his notebook. Word for word. Then he and his spotty girlfriend left. They were both looking pleased as they rode away. And I wished I'd kept my big mouth shut. The Press always make the most of any story in Greenvale. In our town any news is big news.

I suppose things could have been worse though. So far there were no crowds to gape at us. The three kids from number ten came to visit every few minutes, but they did not come close. Miss Gerkin was still sniffing behind the hedge and a group of women kept on walking past pulling empty shopping trolleys. But we could cope with all that.

I just hoped things would stay quiet. Park Road doesn't really lead anywhere. It's on the edge of town. So nothing much happens at the best of times. (Sometimes I wonder if that's why Gran *makes* things happen.)

I spun round as a twig hit my ear. Gran has a very good aim. 'Charlie, I'm hungry. Go and fetch pencil and paper,' she said.

I stared up at her. 'You can't eat pencil and paper.'

Gran snorted. 'Hurry up! Before it gets too dark to see.'

I ran indoors and found a stub of pencil and some paper. By the time I got back outside the street lights were on.

'Now listen carefully, Charlie,' said Gran. 'I want you to write down what I tell you. It's a list of all the things I need.'

I groaned out loud. 'There's nothing you need in a tree, Gran.'

Wrong again. She needed just about everything. And more. It took me quite a while to write the list. When it was finished it looked like this:

reading glasses
book
newspaper
knitting plus spare ball wool
torch

blanket
pillow
woolly hat
pen and notepad
flask of hot tea
cheese and onion sandwiches

It took me even longer to collect all the things together. But Spindle our dog was glad of the company. He had been indoors since Gran first went up. Too scared to come out, poor thing. At first I couldn't find him. But then he came out from under the stairs. He'd been hiding in a pile of rubber boots. When he is scared he likes the smell of rubber. I don't know why. Our vet says he is a dog with problems. Deep, doggy problems. That's why I love him so much. (I mean Spindle, not the vet!).

Outside again there was a difficult job to be faced. The job of getting the things up to Gran. It took a fair bit of working out. But in the end I made a kind of pulley. It's amazing what you can do with a length of washing line and some wire coat hangers. All Gran's things were put into a plastic washing basket. Then Gran hauled the basket up. It worked very well, and Gran was pleased. She said my time at Tech had not been wasted after all. A second Brunel. That's what she called me. But maybe that was overdoing it.

The thought of Tech reminded me of my mates. By now they would be biking across Somerset, racing towards the sunset. Soon they would reach the coast. All that sea and sand. Lucky lot! I bet none of them would have stayed with a Gran up a tree. On a Saturday too! Best night of the week.

'The tea's a bit weak,' said Gran suddenly, from up above.

'Hard luck,' I said.

'But the sandwiches look nice,' she added.

I looked up at Gran. She was unpacking the washing basket. Framed by leaves. In the orange glow of the street light. Just like an old painting.

I walked up the garden path and made sure that the cover was firmly on my bike. It was quiet everywhere now. The sky was black and the heat kept on.

'You think I'm mad, don't you, Charlie,' said Gran, when I got back to the tree.

I shrugged. 'You're not mad. You're just stubborn!'

I paced up and down the grass for a moment. Yawning my head off. Then I turned and went towards the house. Gran had all she needed.

There was no point in staying outside. I was tired. It had been a long, hot day.

'Goodnight, boy. Sleep well,' called Gran as I went indoors and shut the front door.

Up in my attic bedroom I opened the windows wide. I tried not to look out. I had seen enough of Gran for one day. I fell into bed and the dog fell in on top of me. The town clock began to strike. It could have been eleven o'clock. Or twelve. Or maybe only ten. Who was counting? As I drifted off to sleep I could hear Gran's teeth clicking out in the tree. She was chewing her cheese and onion sandwiches.

5

The next morning we had chips for breakfast. Cold chips. Ruby sent them. She's a friend of Gran's and she works at the local fish and chip shop.

While we were eating our chips the vicar called. He had heard about Gran living in a tree. It had not surprised him, but it had worried him. He arrived laughing, showing dozens of big teeth. He was wearing a white straw sun-hat.

'Enjoying your picnic, I see,' he said.

I offered him a chip. He said no thank you, not at the moment. As he spoke he stepped back. I tried to warn him – but too late. There was a great crash as he landed flat on his back.

When he stood up he staggered a bit. Then he grunted a bit. Then he grinned. 'Silly me for not seeing the ladder hiding in the grass,' he said.

Gran said, dryly, 'You were looking up when you should have been looking down, Vicar.'

He nodded. Then he smiled again, giving Gran

the full benefit of his buck teeth. 'I was looking at you, my dear,' he said.

Gran blushed. I felt in the way. So I turned to go indoors. But the vicar stopped me. 'I must help with your problem,' he said. 'But how can I help? How? How? How?'

I just looked at him. He was good on questions. Pity he didn't have a few answers.

Gran chimed in. 'I'm not coming down until the Council promise to leave the trees alone. So don't waste your breath making plans for me.'

The vicar nodded. Like a wise old sage. As if he agreed with every word. No wonder his flower-arranging classes were so popular. He had a way with women. I think the women would still have flocked if his classes were for boot-arranging.

The vicar and Gran chatted for a while. With him gazing up and her gazing down. Then he called out to me, 'I think you are doing a grand job looking after your grandmother.'

I nodded. I had to agree with him. It was the truth.

'But your grandmother needs friends at a time like this,' he said. Then he winked and added, 'Women need women.'

I stared at him. What was he on about?

He gave a toothy grin. 'I'll get some of our

ladies to visit. As soon as I can.'

I thanked him and told him not to bother. The last thing I wanted was a gaggle of old women round the tree. But he insisted. 'It's the least I can do,' he said.

True to his word, he sent three women along. They arrived halfway through the morning. Each of them brought a gift. One of them, dressed in red satin, was Ruby from the chip shop. I tried to escape – but not in time. The women fussed over me like three hens sharing one chick. I nearly died. They had such loud voices. And they called me such soppy names. Such as dear boy, and sweet boy, and poor boy. I hated it.

By now people were peering through their windows. And a small group had gathered in the street. The three kids from number ten were singing their rude song again and Miss Gerkin was sniffing behind the hedge. I ran indoors as soon as I could. I must have broken the sprint record.

It was another boiling hot day. My bedroom smelled of whippet and yesterday's socks. But it was the best place to be. I felt safe there. Until the noise began to drift up from the garden. Four women all talking at once make an awful row. There was Ruby shouting upwards, and Gran shouting downwards while the other two shouted everything twice because the battery had gone on Ruby's hearing aid. I cringed and covered my ears. Our neighbours could hear all our business. In stereo!

I flopped on to my bed. If it hadn't been so hot I would have closed my windows. But I needed what fresh air there was. Our house is hottest up high under the roof. I closed my eyes for a moment. Sleep would be an escape. Death would be bliss. But it was no good. There was no peace at all. The noise outside was growing. Gran was yelling her head off now – telling everyone about her night in the tree. She said she had seen a big brown rat, and it was awful.

Ruby asked what was awful about seeing a cat.

'Rat! Rat!' yelled Gran. 'I saw a rat!'

Ruby still did not understand. She said she liked cats.

I sat up and looked out of my window. One of the women was doing a funny walk and stroking her whiskers. I think she was pretending to be a rat. But Ruby just looked at her, deadpan, as if she was touched by the heat.

'It was as big as a dog, with black beady eyes! It was nasty, really nasty,' said Gran. She then went on about the way the rat had crawled along the branch and sat on her slipper . . . and crawled up her leg . . . and pounced . . . over her shoulder.

Gran is good at telling a tale. But she lies like a pig in straw. I knew that Gran had not seen a rat. And Gran knew that she had not seen a rat. It was probably a squirrel she had seen, but a rat makes a far better story. The trees in Park Road are often visited by squirrels. I just felt sorry for the poor squirrel who had bumped into Gran. It must have had a fright seeing Gran without her teeth in.

I groaned. My name was being called. It was Gran, calling me to go out and work the pulley. There were things to be hauled up. One of the women had brought roses for Gran. Another had brought a large jam tart. And Ruby had brought a piece of cooked cod.

It did not take long to fix the washing basket and the pulley. Soon Gran was hauling away and within minutes she had unpacked the roses, the tart and the cod.

People standing around began clapping as Gran made a speech of thanks. Then the three women left, still shouting because of Ruby's hearing aid. And I was glad. Glad to see the back of them.

Gran was smiling. Sitting up in the tree with

her gifts. She sniffed at the roses. 'Nice roses,' she said. She nibbled at the edge of the tart. 'Tasty tart,' she said. Then, suddenly, Ruby's cooked cod came flying through the air. It landed with a flop at my feet.

'Oh, what a shame. I've dropped it,' said Gran. I looked up at her. I could see she was trying to hide a smile. She had always hated fish. And as for cold cooked cod – it would have been easier to make her eat cold cooked snake!

I called Spindle. He was not a bit fussy. He ate Ruby's fish in three quick gulps. Then he sat on the grass and howled. I thought perhaps he had got a fish bone stuck somewhere. But then I understood why he was so upset. He hated seeing Gran up in a tree.

I knew just how he felt. If I'd been a dog I would have sat down and howled with him. I bent down to stroke him and have a quiet word in his ear. Then the sound of giggling came from behind me. It was the three little girls from number ten. Bless their hearts. They were giggling so much I thought they might burst – with luck. Whether they were giggling at me or Spindle I don't know. I did not wait to find out. I ran indoors. I needed an ice-cold bath to stop me blowing my top!

6

By midday the road was quieter. Some of our neighbours were out, doing the usual Sunday jobs. Mowing lawns. Cleaning cars. Catching up on gossip.

I dozed in the shade of the tree with Spindle flopped at my feet. Gran was up in the branches, knitting. She seemed quite happy in her own little world of birds and sunshine. I could smell dinner. But it wasn't ours. I knew we would end up with sandwiches again. Cheese and onion sandwiches. That's the only meal I can do without a fuss.

'Ahoy there! Enemy coming!' yelled Gran, suddenly. I jumped up. Gran was leaning out of the tree. She had a rolled-up paper held to one eye. Trying to do a Nelson. Only Nelson did not wear pink slippers.

I looked along the road. A police car was on its way and when it stopped two policemen got out. The same two as before: the tall one and the heavy one. They slammed their car doors. Slam!

Slam! Then they came trudging across the grass towards me.

Too late! There was a terrific crash as the heavy one fell. Flat out. Over the ladder. Face down on the grass. It took him a minute or two to untangle himself. I tried to help. But Spindle got there first. And he licked the policeman's face all over.

I waited as the policeman brushed himself down. 'Someone should do something about that ladder,' he muttered. Then he glared at me, and added, 'Something should be done about that dog too!'

The men asked to speak to me indoors. Which made Gran angry. She hates being left out of anything. I could tell Gran was getting into a real bad mood by the way she was standing up and shaking the branches. She looked like a bad-tempered chimp. Only not quite so hairy.

Indoors the policemen told me they were getting a doctor for Gran. I tried to make them see that Gran was not ill but they insisted. They said it was their duty.

As the police car drove off Gran pelted it with toffees. She did the same to the doctor's car when it arrived half an hour later.

I was sorry to see the new man. Not our usual doctor who is used to Gran and her funny ways.

This doctor had bright red hair and a beard to match. His name was Doctor Mackenzie. As he crossed the grass I warned him just in time about the ladder hidden there. He said he was grateful for the warning.

'It's my grandmother you've come to see. She's up there,' I said.

Then he peered up into the tree. 'Good morning,' he shouted.

Gran nodded and gave him a royal wave of the hand.

He stroked his beard and thought for a moment. Then he said, 'May I put the ladder up? I would like to climb up and examine you.'

Gran smiled sweetly. 'Yes Doctor. Do come up.'

I was surprised. More than surprised. Shocked! Gran had not allowed anyone to go up before now. Not even me. So why had she changed all of a sudden. Why was her mood all sweetness and light now?

I helped the doctor to lift up the ladder. Then, when it was in the right place the doctor began to climb.

I walked away and sat on the grass, sipping cider. The sun was still beating down. More waiting. More wondering. But I had hopes. This could be the end of Gran's protest if Doctor Mackenzie could get her to come down. Then we could all get back to normal.

There was fast breathing beside me. It was Spindle. He looked sad as he licked my hand. He hated all the upset and fuss. I sank back on the warm grass and closed my eyes. If only I could be out on my bike. Just me and the open road. With the bike going flat out. Throttle wide open, and miles of fresh air and freedom. There was still a chance. If Gran came down from the tree now I could be out by two o'clock.

Suddenly there was a scream. Like Tarzan with toothache. I jumped up and the dog shot indoors. Then came a terrific crash. Doctor Mackenzie had come down. The hard way.

I rushed to the foot of the tree. He was lying on his back, groaning. 'Are you all right, Doctor?' I said.

If looks could have killed I'd be dead now. 'Of course I'm not all right!' he screeched.

'What happened?' I asked.

He pointed to Gran, who was still up in the tree. 'Ask her! Ask your grandmother what happened!'

I looked up at Gran. 'What happened?'

Gran shrugged. 'The doctor would not go

down when I told him to go. So I just helped him on his way a bit.'

I yelled at Gran. 'But you can't just push people away when they are on top of ladders!'

'I can, and I did,' said Gran. 'He told me he did not care about trees. He said he did not care if our beech tree turned into firewood. So I got rid of him.'

The doctor struggled to sit up. He shook a fist at Gran. 'You might have killed me. I shall sue you.'

Gran's answer was quick. 'If you sue me I shall report you!'

As I helped the doctor to his feet he called Gran a ruddy pest. Poor thing. I couldn't help feeling sorry for him.

When we were on our own again I sat down on the front doorstep. I needed time to think. I could see no answer to all this. Gran had been up in the tree for almost twenty-four hours. She was no nearer coming down now than at the start. And there was no let-up in the heatwave. I felt fed-up. Really fed-up.

I jumped as a soft voice sounded in front of me. A girl's voice. 'Your Gran is a stubborn one, isn't she?'

I looked up into brown eyes. It was Tessa, the

new girl in my class at Tech. I was used to seeing her in the classroom and the workshop but she looked different now. Even nicer than before. I couldn't think what to say, so I said, 'Gran is as stubborn as a mule at times.'

Tessa smiled a slow smile. I felt the back of my neck going red. (I've got the sort of neck that can't keep a secret.) Then she said, 'Even mules get hungry,' and she handed me a box.

Then she was gone. Running along Park Road. Too shy to stay. She was wearing a white shirt, blue jeans, and flip-flop sandals tied on with string. I watched her until she reached the corner. Then I opened the box she had given me which was full of home-made cakes. I had not had time to thank her.

7

I kept smelling roast beef. But the smell was all we got. While other people sat down to Sunday dinner Gran and I ate apples and rock cakes. When Miss Gerkin stepped into her garden I thought she might be bringing us food. But no such luck. She was only interested in spraying her greenfly. As she marched from rose bush to rose bush she glared at me. As if it was all my fault! Then she said one word, 'Disgusting,' before marching indoors.

Gran was missing her proper meals. I could tell by the way she made up little poems about tripe. On and on she went about hot tripe, pie and onions piled high. Her poems made me sweat. It was a new form of torture on such a hot day. I was glad when she finally dozed off to sleep.

At two o'clock a coach drew up. It stopped not far from our tree. About a dozen people got out. They were all carrying boards and folding-chairs. I watched as they unfolded their chairs and put up their boards. This was the first time I had seen an open-air art class.

The woman in charge beamed a smile. She had blue hair piled up like a cottage loaf. She was wearing a blue smock and a long blue skirt. She had blue lipstick and finger-nails to match. I stepped back a bit as she came charging across the grass. She flew over the ladder like a big, blue bird.

'We are here to draw this tree,' she cried. 'It's our last chance before it is cut down. It's such a wonderful tree.'

I was not sure what to say. So I said nothing. None of the crowd had noticed Gran up on her perch. And Gran was keeping quiet. Too quiet, for my liking. I had a feeling that something was about to happen. And it did! Gran waited until the class was ready to start drawing. Then she let one skinny leg dangle through the branches. It just hung there in mid-air with a pink slipper on the end of it. It was awful!

One lady screamed and a little grey man fell off his chair in surprise. The blue lady ran to me. 'Is that an old woman up in the tree? Or am I dreaming?' she said.

'You're dreaming,' I said. But she did not believe me.

Two of them begged for tea. It was the only cure for shock, they said.

'Make it hot and sweet!' yelled Gran as I went indoors to begin the big brew-up.

We didn't have enough cups for all of them but I managed to find a few tin mugs – and some plastic beakers from the bathroom. And I found some biscuits which Mum had hidden away. The whole thing didn't take long. Soon they were all happy again, sipping tea in the shade of the tree.

As the arty crowd sipped, Gran told them about her fight with the Council. She said if our road were made any wider it would be used as a short-cut across town. Lorries, tractors, cattle-trucks. It wouldn't be safe for children any more. There would be no peace, no bird-song. Just diesel fumes and noise. The Council were trying to turn our road into a motorway – but she was going to stop them. Even if it killed her!

The people nodded in all the right places. They seemed interested. But whether they were really on Gran's side, or just grateful for the tea, I could not tell. When Gran stopped speaking the blue lady stood up. Her eyes were shining and her piled-up hair was wobbling. 'I think you are a very brave person,' she said to Gran.

'Very brave. Very brave indeed,' said everyone.

'The town planners are fools! I'll show you

what I think of them!' went on the blue lady. She then marched across the grass and tripped over the ladder.

No-one said a word. We just waited as she picked herself up and began marching again. This time she went along Park Road to where a Council lorry was parked. She kicked the wheel of the lorry. Then she kicked it again. Hard.

'Bravo,' shouted the little grey man.

'Well done,' shouted the rest of the crowd.

'Can I have another cup of tea?' said the coach driver.

Everyone clapped and cheered as the blue lady tried to march back. She had stubbed her toe rather badly. But she put on a brave smile.

Back at the tree the crowd decided to have a meeting. The blue lady took charge because she had the loudest voice. She said it would be a good idea to start a petition. So everyone stood in line, taking it in turns to sign their names on a large piece of art paper. Some of our neighbours signed their names too, and for a while people stood and chatted in the sunshine. I looked up at Gran. She grinned down from the tree and gave the thumbs-up sign. Even the dog was in a good mood. He was busy licking out the cups.

At four o'clock the arty crowd packed up and

left. They were singing as their coach drove away.

I turned and began to clear up the mess. There were cups all over the garden.

'Thanks Charlie. Thanks for making the tea,' said Gran.

I did not answer her. I was too busy looking for Mum's pink tooth-mug. Then I came across a beaker full of money. The art class must have had a collection.

I didn't get a chance to count the cash. Gran was suddenly leaning out of the tree, doing her Nelson act again. 'Enemy ships on the horizon, Charlie. Man the guns!' she yelled.

8

There were five council men. All wearing dark suits and deep frowns. These were not the workmen in plastic helmets who came before. These were desk men with brief-cases. They came striding across the grass like soldiers. Left right left right – then crash! The leader tripped over the ladder and there was a pile-up.

We were off to a bad start. I said sorry five times. Then I called off the dog and the men got up.

The leader glared at me. He had bushy eyebrows and a bald head. (Bald but for a few hairs combed across the dome.) Then he glared up at Gran. His eyes were small and glinting, like currants in a bun.

'Good afternoon, Madam,' he called up to Gran. His voice was flat. He seemed to speak through his nose.

Gran did not answer. She was eating an apple.

The man walked round the tree. Then he

45

snapped, 'I am from the Council. My name is Mr Conch.'

Gran spat out a pip. 'That's your problem,' she said.

One of the men laughed. The laugh was cut short.

'We have come to order you to get out of that tree!' said Mr Conch.

The man behind Mr Conch chipped in. 'Yes, we order you out of that tree now!'

Gran was so angry you could see the spit on the air. 'Listen you,' she said. 'You can't order me to do anything! Here I am. And here I stay!'

Mr Conch took a deep breath and smoothed his seven hairs. 'You can't stay up there, Madam.'

'I can, and I will!' said Gran. 'I will stay in this tree until I have a promise from you. I want a promise that you will leave our trees alone.'

Mr Conch made an ugly face. (He did not need to try very hard.) His mouth was a thin hard line as he opened his briefcase. 'I have here a piece of paper,' he said.

'Big deal!' said Gran.

He began to read from the paper. 'Part one, section three states that. . . .'

Gran stopped him in mid-drone. 'I don't care

about section three. I care about trees,' she said.

Mr Conch snapped his case shut. He was breathing hard now. Trying to control his anger.

'Now look here my good woman,' he began.

Gran snapped. 'I am not your good woman!'

Mr Conch gulped and rolled his eyes a bit. Then he began shouting at the top of his voice. 'You silly woman! Wasting my time! If you don't come down now, this minute, I shall come up and drag you down!'

Gran's answer was not in words. She flung down a tin plate. It hit Mr Conch in the briefcase. He stepped back. So did the rest of his gang. And they all held up their briefcases. Like shields. While Gran pelted them with apple cores.

Mr Conch's face was purple with rage. But he did not give up. He walked over to the ladder and began to lift it.

'Stop, stop,' I yelled. I could hear Gran making a sound like a snarl. I thought she was going to have a fit. I ran across the grass. 'Go away,' I said to Mr Conch. 'Go away and leave us alone!'

He dropped the ladder and turned on me. 'Listen sonny boy, just stay out of this. Okay?'

His face was so close I could smell his breath. It stank of old cigars. I did not move. I stood there, eye to eye with him. Then I said firmly, 'You had better go. You are upsetting my grandmother. And when she's upset I'm upset. And when I'm upset there's usually trouble.'

One of the other men sprang forward. He was sweating like a pig. 'Trouble? We've had nothing *but* trouble since your stupid grandmother climbed that tree! The phones have been ringing non-stop. We should be off duty today. It's Sunday! But people won't let us rest. That woman is crazy! She should be locked up!'

He took a step forward. I took a step back. He took another step forward. I took another step back. Then crash! I fell over the ladder.

The man stood over me and laughed. I sat up. He nudged me back with his knees. This happened twice. While I boiled inside and out.

Then Gran shouted from above. 'Hit him, Charlie! Go on, hit him!'

I got up quickly. It was all very well for Gran. She was not standing where I was standing. From where I stood the view was not good. (The man was as big as a bus.)

I started to go indoors. But Mr Conch ran to stop me. He grabbed hold of my arm and swung me round. And that was where he made his big mistake. Spindle flew at him.

'Take your leg out of our dog's mouth,'

shouted Gran.

Mr Conch was sweating hard as he tried to shake the dog off. But Spindle hung on. (Spindle's teeth might be old, but they're still in good working order.) Then Mr Conch swung his briefcase and hit Spindle sideways on.

Spindle flew indoors, yelping. I followed after. But I only got as far as the front door. I was held by two of the men while Mr Conch limped across the lawn towards me. When he reached me he was like a wild thing, shiny with sweat and showing his rotten teeth. 'I've had enough of you and your family,' he sneered. 'So I'm going to teach you a lesson. No-one makes a fool of me and gets away with it.'

As he spoke his friends closed in. They stood round me in a circle. I had no way of escape.

'Hit them! Go on Charlie, hit them!' called Gran. She had to be joking! Me against five? I would have ended up like that cold cod if I'd tried. Splat! All over the path!

I looked across the lawn. Wishing and wondering. Wishing I was safe up in a tree like Gran. Wondering whether to make a run for it. And that's when I first saw the TV crew! They were on the other side of the road, filming every move we made.

Mr Conch saw the look of surprise on my face. He spun round. And when *he* saw the cameras his face was a picture!

In two seconds flat he was out of our garden with no sign of a limp now. Just as fast, his four henchmen followed after him. I laughed at them. They looked so scared now, clinging together. Trying to hide behind the tree. But they could not escape the camera. The TV crew soon closed in. And there were some lovely close-up shots. There was one of Mr Conch peeping round his briefcase. And one of Gran's legs dangling. And one of Spindle tripping over the ladder.

Questions were asked. Answers were given. Mr Conch against Gran – all filmed and recorded. First Gran gave her view. Then Mr Conch gave his view. Then the newsman asked me what I thought. And my mind went blank. So I gave a sickly grin and said 'No comment.'

Suddenly there was music coming along Park Road. It was beat music, heavy on the drums. I looked and saw the sun glinting on the red and gold uniforms. It was Greenvale town band, out in full strength. The TV crew spun their cameras round to meet it. And people came rushing out of their houses.

The band was leading a long line of marchers.

The marchers were carrying a banner which said 'SAVE OUR TREES'. The vicar was at the head of the line. He was followed by Ruby and her friends. After that came the blue lady and the members of her art class. Then there were neighbours, and a lot more people from the town. People I'd never met before.

'Thank you!' called out Gran, as the crowd passed our tree. The vicar blew her a kiss. He made quite a picture with the last of the sunset glinting on his buck teeth.

At the end of the line came the two policemen. The two we already knew – the heavy one and the tall one. They were strolling along, chatting. Looking relaxed without their jackets on. It's funny, really. It wasn't until I saw them with their sleeves rolled up that I realized they were ordinary people.

9

Mr Conch and his men had no choice. They went straight to the town hall to hold a public meeting. It looked as though Gran had won the battle of the tree. But she still would not come down. She said she would come down when she saw a written promise from Mr Conch. She wanted a proper signed statement that the trees would be left standing.

I watched her as she sat waiting up in the branches. She was knitting in the orange glow of the streetlight. Mr Conch was due back at eight o'clock with the statement. So really Gran could have come down now. But she was still the same as ever. Stubborn to the very end.

Gran looked tired. More than tired. She looked ill. I wondered whether to put the ladder up and go and sit with her. But I did not fancy being stabbed with a size nine needle.

I went indoors and made tea and sandwiches. Cheese and onion sandwiches again. Spindle was under the stairs, trembling from his nose to his tail. The day had been too much for him. And now he had a sort of doom-gloom look on his face. As if he sensed a storm brewing. I felt it too when I went outside again. The air was thick and heavy. The garden seemed to smell far too sweet. Gran said she could not face any more cold food. She did not even want a cup of tea. That worried me more than anything. I have never known Gran refuse a 'cuppa'. I looked up quickly. Gran was huddled up now. Wrapped in her knitting. Shivering. Looking sick.

'Gran! What's wrong?' I yelled.

She said something about hot tripe and onions. But it was hard for me to hear her. A breeze had sprung up. And there was the rumble of thunder on the other side of town.

A car drew up. It was Mr Conch. He came towards me waving a piece of paper. The paper was signed, just as Gran had wanted. It was a written statement that the trees in Park Road would be left for the people to enjoy them. He did not stay long. Just long enough to tell me about the public meeting. There were new plans now. A ring-road would be built round the edge of town. So Park Road would stay exactly the same as it always was. Green . . . and peaceful . . . and lined with beech trees.

The wind was getting stronger, rustling the branches, bringing leaves and twigs down. I waved the paper and shouted to Gran. It was good news. Now she would be able to come down to earth. Now we could all get back to normal.

But Gran did not answer. She just sat up in the branches, nodding. Like a rag doll. Her eyes were half closed. Was she dozing? Or playing one of her usual tricks?

'Gran! Gran!' I yelled.

No answer. I ran and lifted the ladder out of the grass. It was heavy. I could feel the sweat running down my back. I set the ladder in place and climbed up quickly. Something was wrong with Gran. Very wrong. She was too still. Too quiet. When I reached her I could see she was propped against a branch. She looked even worse than I had thought. She was asleep. But it was not a normal sleep. She was breathing in short gasps. Her face was as hot as fire. Her hands cold as ice. I tried to lift her, but she was a dead-weight. I felt suddenly quite sick.

Within seconds I was down out of the tree and running. Running like the wind to get to a phone box. I knew there was a phone box in the next road. I only hoped it was not out of order. I needed help. And fast!

A police car drew up beside me. It was the tall one and the heavy one on patrol. I told the men about Gran being ill. They told me not to worry, and they took over. The tall one who was driving did a quick U-turn while his mate called for the Fire Service on his radio. Then the car was on its way back to the tree, leaving me to follow behind.

As I ran the first drops of rain fell. Then the downpour began. And the awful heat seemed to get worse for a while. It felt as though the earth was on fire. Even the rain was warm. Then came the lightning and all the trees turned silver-white against the dark night. I wondered whether Gran was still asleep. She hated storms. She'd be terrified to be stuck in a tree on a night like this.

When I arrived home the two policemen were already up in the tree. Busy. Coping. Doing their first-aid stuff. They were wrapping Gran in a blanket, and using their rolled-up jackets as pillows. There was nothing I could do but watch and wait. I was drenched. Soaked from head to foot. But I hardly noticed. I was too worried about Gran.

There was a loud crack of thunder. Then a small branch hung in mid-air before falling to earth. I was blown back against the garden hedge. The wind was gale-force now. Strong enough to snap the great beech tree in half. For the first time in my life, I felt really afraid.

One of the men called down and told me to wait in the house. But I wanted to be outside. I began to pace round the garden. Round and round in the teeming rain until my eyes were stinging. Then I heard myself saying, 'Please God, don't let Gran die!' I didn't care who heard me!

I could hear the fire engine when it was still a long way off. As it turned into Park Road it was lit by a flash of lightning. Stark red against the black of night. When the wailing siren stopped people came rushing from their houses. 'Where's the fire?' someone shouted. 'There isn't a fire – but I reckon there'll be a funeral,' someone answered.

As soon as the engine was in place things happened very quickly. There were five firemen and each of them had a job to do. A search-light was turned on. A ladder was raised. Then one of the men went up and Gran was lifted safely down to earth. The same man carried Gran into the house. Gran was still asleep, miles away from the here-and-now. She didn't even blink an eyelid as a loud crash of thunder sounded overhead.

The blue light on top of the engine was still flashing. On-off, on-off. Lighting up the faces of the crowd in the road. I shivered. They looked like ghosts in the rain.

Indoors, the tall policeman said to me, 'Make a big pot of tea, Charlie.' He smiled as he said it. His face was dripping wet from the rain. He looked tired.

I went to the kitchen – glad to have a job to do. I could hear the heavy one talking on his two-way radio. He was calling for an ambulance, trying to talk through the crackling of the storm. I stood at the kitchen window and looked out. The sky was still going mad. And the rain kept on tipping down.

10

The hospital kept Gran for twenty-four hours. They said she would get better faster at home. She needed lots and lots of sleep and plenty of hot food. They said she had won her battle – but the battle had almost killed her.

'I reckon we got home just in time,' said my dad.

'Only just in time,' sniffed Mum. They were sitting one on each side of Gran's bed. Gran asleep, propped up by three pillows and our whippet.

It was ten o'clock on the Tuesday morning. Gran's room was full of sunshine and flowers. The windows were wide open and the birds were singing in the tree outside. The milkman had left a single rose in a milk bottle for Gran. (Other flowers had come from neighbours.) And a huge bunch of roses had come from the Police. I was sitting near the door of Gran's room, letting in the visitors. It was like sitting in a flower-shop.

So far, the room held:

the vicar
Ruby and her friends
Mum and Dad
Aunt Brenda from Bristol
the blue lady from the art class
our neighbour, Miss Gerkin
. . . and Gran and me and the dog.

I just hoped the floor would hold up.

The visitors were not in a chatty mood. They were far too worried about Gran.

Ruby blew her nose and dabbed her eyes. 'I do hope Gran will be all right,' she whispered.

Aunt Brenda put an arm round Ruby. 'Don't cry, Ruby,' she said. Then she burst into tears herself.

Mum leaned forward and covered her face with her hands. 'I've got one of my headaches coming,' she said. As she spoke her voice cracked on a high note. Dad reached out a hand to her. Then he drew back, not sure what to do.

I leaned back against the wall and closed my eyes. I *needed* Gran. I had not known how much I needed her until now. She was the one who listened when I had problems. She was the only one who had *time* to listen. And she was the only person in the world to laugh at my jokes. Even when they were corny jokes. If anything happened to Gran . . . if I didn't have Gran. . . .

I jumped up. 'Would anyone like a cup of tea?'

Mum wiped her eyes and smiled. 'Oh, I'd love some tea, Charlie. Thanks very much.'

I opened the door to go out just as another visitor came in. It was my friend, Tessa. She was holding a covered dish.

'I've brought some tripe for Gran,' she said, quietly.

'Some what?' I said.

'Some tripe,' she said. Then she took the lid from the dish and the room was filled with the smell of steaming hot tripe and onions.

Gran smiled in her sleep. Then she moved, and her nose began to twitch. The smell of tripe was wafting into her dreams. Suddenly, she opened her eyes and sat up. 'Tripe. Lovely tripe and onions. I can't wait!'

A cheer went up as Gran began to eat. Then everybody began talking at once. They were all happy now. Ruby was so happy that she cried like a baby. And she didn't stop until the vicar thumped her on the back. Miss Gerkin made a speech. So did the blue lady from the art class. Two different speeches. Both at the same time. Mum and Dad were kissing each other. And while all this was going on, Spindle was whooping it up with Gran's pink slippers on the end of the bed.

Gran carried on eating. We were the only two who were sane. Then Gran glanced up at me. 'Thanks Charlie, for sticking by me. I reckon you're the best grandson a grandmother could ever have.'

I could feel the back of my neck growing bright red. I looked round to see if Tessa was still in the room. But she'd slipped away while no-one was looking.

Ruby offered to make the tea. I went downstairs and out into the garden. The noise from Gran's room was spilling out of the open window. It sounded like a party. I took a deep breath. I was glad it was all over. I felt free again. Everything smelled clean after the rain. I was glad to be alive.

Along the road Council men were at work. Removing their gear. Soon, no-one would even remember the battle of the tree.

I looked up at the great beech tree. It was a hundred years old or more. And Gran had risked her life to give it another hundred years. I wondered if the blackbird on the top branch knew that. He was singing fit to burst. Singing as if it was the last song in the world.

A sudden roar filled Park Road. A convoy of bikes had turned the corner. I ran out to meet them. It was Mick and the gang. Laughing and waving. Happy as kings. I couldn't hear what they were shouting to me. But I got the message. And as I ran to fetch my bike I knew just how that little blackbird felt. As soon as I had the open road I was going to sing! Sing fit to burst – as if it was the last song in the world!